A PLACE CALLED
HIROSHIMA

A PLACE CALLED HIROSHI

Text by
BETTY JEAN LIFTON

Photographs by
EIKOH HOSOE

MA

KODANSHA INTERNATIONAL LTD.
Tokyo, New York, San Francisco

CREDITS

Photographs:
Pp. 22–23, three minutes after the explosion, material returned from the U.S. Armed Forces Institute of Pathology and now in the possession of the Hiroshima Peace Culture Foundation; p. 25, two or three minutes after the explosion, photo by Seizo Yamada; pp. 26–27, around 11:00 A.M., August 6, 1945, photo by Yoshito Matsushige; pp. 32–33, early October, 1945, photo by Shigeo Hayashi; p. 60 (top), August 7, 1945, p. 63, August 1945, photo by Masayoshi Onuka; p. 60 (bottom), August 7, 1945, photo by Yotsugi Kawahara; p. 61, late August, 1945, photo by The Association of Photographers of the Hiroshima Atomic Bombing.
Paintings:
Pp. 28–29, 30–31: section, "Fire (II)," 1950; p. 34: section, "Bamboo Thicket (VII)," 1954—from *The Hiroshima Panels* (180 cm × 720cm) by Iri Maruki and Toshi Maruki.

CHRONOLOGY OF PHOTOGRAPHS:

Ca. 1935: p. 38
March, 1941: p. 57
Ca. 1946: p. 109
October 14, 1954: p. 48
March 16, 1955: p. 47
1957: p. 115
May 19, 1967: pp. 85, 104–105
May 20, 1967: p. 73, 75
May 21, 1967: p. 93, 113
August 6, 1967: pp. 43, 46, 56, 91
August 8, 1967: pp. 122–123
August 10, 1967: pp. 87, 88–89
August 15, 1967: p. 59
August 20, 1967: pp. 68–69, 71
August 27, 1967: pp. 81, 82–83
August 28, 1967: p. 65
August 6, 1983: title page, pp. 128–129, 130–131, 145
April 4, 1984: p. 117
April 5, 1984: pp. 18–19
April 7, 1984: pp. 79, 106–107, 110–111
April 8, 1984: pp. 36–37, 76, 112, 119, 121, 134–135
August 5, 1984: pp. 101, 102, 103, 140–141
August 6, 1984: pp. 6, 124–125, 126–127, 132–133, 139, 146–147, 148–149, 150–151
August 7, 1984: pp. 39, 40–41, 44, 45, 51 (top and bottom), 53, 55, 66–67, 94
August 8, 1984: pp. 20–21
August 10, 1984: pp. 8–9, 136–137 (both), 142–143
October 10, 1984: pp. 10–11, 12–13, 14–15, 16, 50, 97, 98–99

Distributed in the United States by Kodansha International/USA Ltd., through Harper & Row, Publishers, Inc., 10 East 53rd Street, New York, New York 10022.

Published by Kodansha International Ltd., 12–21 Otowa 2-chome, Bunkyo-ku, Tokyo 112 and Kodansha International/USA Ltd., with offices at 10 East 53rd Street, New York, New York 10022 and The Hearst Building, 5 Third Street, Suite No. 430, San Francisco, California 94103.

Printed in Japan.
First edition, 1985.
Second printing, 1985.

Library of Congress Cataloging in Publication Data

Lifton, Betty Jean.
A place called Hiroshima.
1. Hiroshima-shi (Japan)—Bombardment, 1945.
I. Title.
D767.25.H6L39 1985 940.54'26 84–48127
ISBN 0–87011–649–5
ISBN 4–7700–1149–0 (in Japan)

For the children of Hiroshima
and the world.

To begin with—

This place you've come to see called Hiroshima
is no one place.

There are many places, each bearing that name.
One is located in the past.
One in the present.
One in the future.

Understand—

The legendary place that you seek
is not located on a map.

It is a state of mind.

Still you return over the years looking for Hiroshima.
And always you ask:
How will I know when I arrive?

Is there anything still there?
Is there anyone who can remember?
Is there anyone who can forget?

They say it is Hiroshima—

Yet, it does not seem possible that this thriving port city in western Japan had been laid waste by an atomic bomb on August 6, 1945.

You are unprepared for its beauty. Nestled against low mountains and opening out to the miniature islands of the Inland Sea, it exudes the charm of a small provincial town. The Ota River still winds lazily through it, its seven fingers weaving together the marshy deltas on which it lies.

You have to remind yourself that Hiroshima was once an inbred castle town where the Emperor's troops were garrisoned. Its castle served as a military headquarters. Its ships pointed toward China and the conquest of Asia. Its streets meandered without plan into a maze of winding alleyways created haphazardly over the centuries, until an atomic bomb catapulted it into the nuclear age.

Now resurrected as a twentieth century city, its broad boulevards set off tall municipal buildings, modern hotels, and fashionable department stores.

Seek out the castle—

It, too, was resurrected, but out of ferroconcrete rather than those old sensual wooden beams, which once made it a national treasure.

Serving now as a museum exhibiting samurai armor, the castle sits, like the rest of the city, over the ashes of those who perished by a weapon undreamed of by those ancient warriors. Its vista: the low income housing projects built for the A-Bomb victims.

You learn that most of Hiroshima's population is made up of outsiders who swarmed in from Japan's former colonies after the war to take advantage of the frontier conditions.

Those newcomers gave Hiroshima its energy to rebuild its shipyards and industries, which now churn out automobiles and sewing needles, rather than

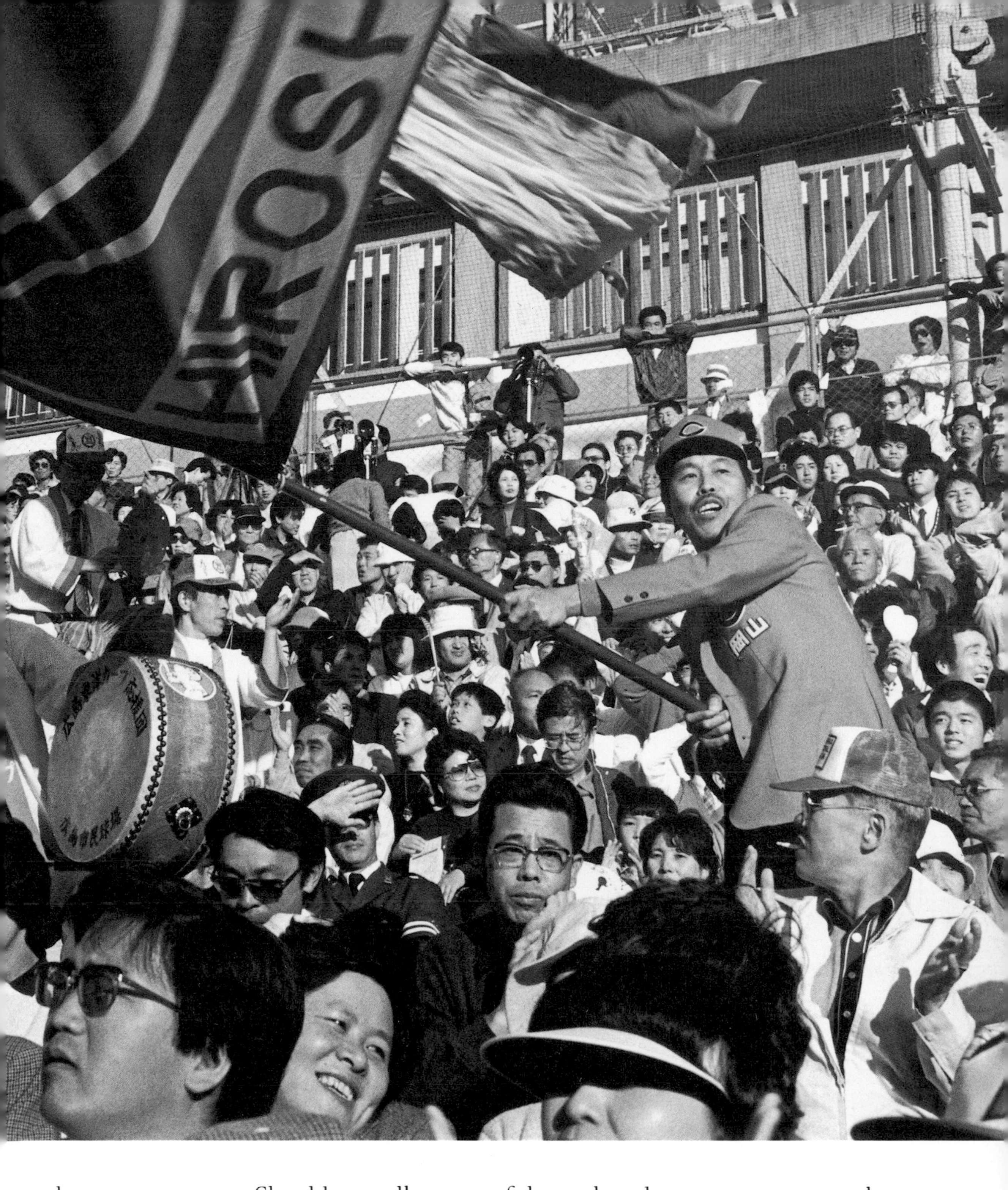

heavy armaments. Should you talk to any of them, they do not seem to remember the past. They would rather speak of the Hiroshima Carps, the baseball team that is the pride of the city.

You think, perhaps, after all; it is possible to forget.

祝 V4我らのカープ!
金座街
May's
ELZA
SIMON
スポーツセンター
レコード
寿光堂
KINZAGAI

By day you wander through the arcaded shopping centers of the place called Hiroshima.

At night you relax in the entertainment area where men go after work to drink with their friends, entertain their clients, or banter with the bar girls. You go there to eat the famous Hiroshima oysters and drink its delicious rice wine, *saké*.

You ask a *Mama-san* why she named her bar "Riddle."

"It sounds exotic," she says. "And it seems to pose a question about life."

You learn that she was fourteen when the bomb killed her mother and sister. She still carries the scars from the flying glass that slashed her body.

"I often think that my life would have been different if my mother had

lived," she tells you. "But I don't talk about such things with my customers. They come here to forget their troubles, not to hear mine. They want me smiling and gay."

And she adds as she pours you yet another cup of *saké*: "We could not live in this world if somehow we could not manage to forget."

How much to remember, how much to forget? This is the dilemma that Hiroshima—like the rest of the world—still struggles with.

Yet you will find that most of Hiroshima's ninety thousand survivors remember only too well. For them it is still 8:15 in the morning. The all clear has just sounded. Families are going on with their breakfast. Small children are leaving for school, older ones to join the "volunteer" demolition squads in the center of town. Men and women are on their way to work, or already at their desks. Soldiers are reporting to duty at military posts or at the busy port.

A B-29 suddenly appears overhead.

It is the Enola Gay, destined to share the immortality of the atomic bomb it now releases eighteen hundred and fifty feet over the center of the city.

There is a blinding flash of light, a blast of searing heat, and then an ominous multicolored cloud rising like a poisonous mushroom into the sky, its fiery roots lashing out with the intensity of a tornado.

Those closest to the hypocenter above which the bomb explodes are incinerated on the spot, or perish in the flames that whip through the streets. Others within a mile and a half radius of the blast will succumb shortly from flash burns and the intense dosage of radiation.

The strength of the *pikadon*—the flash boom, as the Japanese call the bomb—was equivalent to thirteen thousand tons of TNT.

It occurs to you that bombs exist today with a thousand times that destructive power.

The survivors, who will become known as *hibakusha*, explosion-affected people, do not understand what has happened to them. They stagger about half naked, their clothing ripped from their bodies, their skin shredded, their facial features melted beyond recognition.

They think they are in some Buddhist hell.

Those who are strong enough flee east to the hilltop of Hijiyama and look down on what was once their city.

It seems impossible.

Hiroshima has disappeared.

Within an instant the bomb destroyed sixty thousand houses in a three mile radius. The flimsy wooden structures collapsed on their inhabitants in the fury of the blast and were consumed in the wildfires that came tearing through. Only the shells of a few concrete structures were left to bear testimony that once there were inhabitants here.

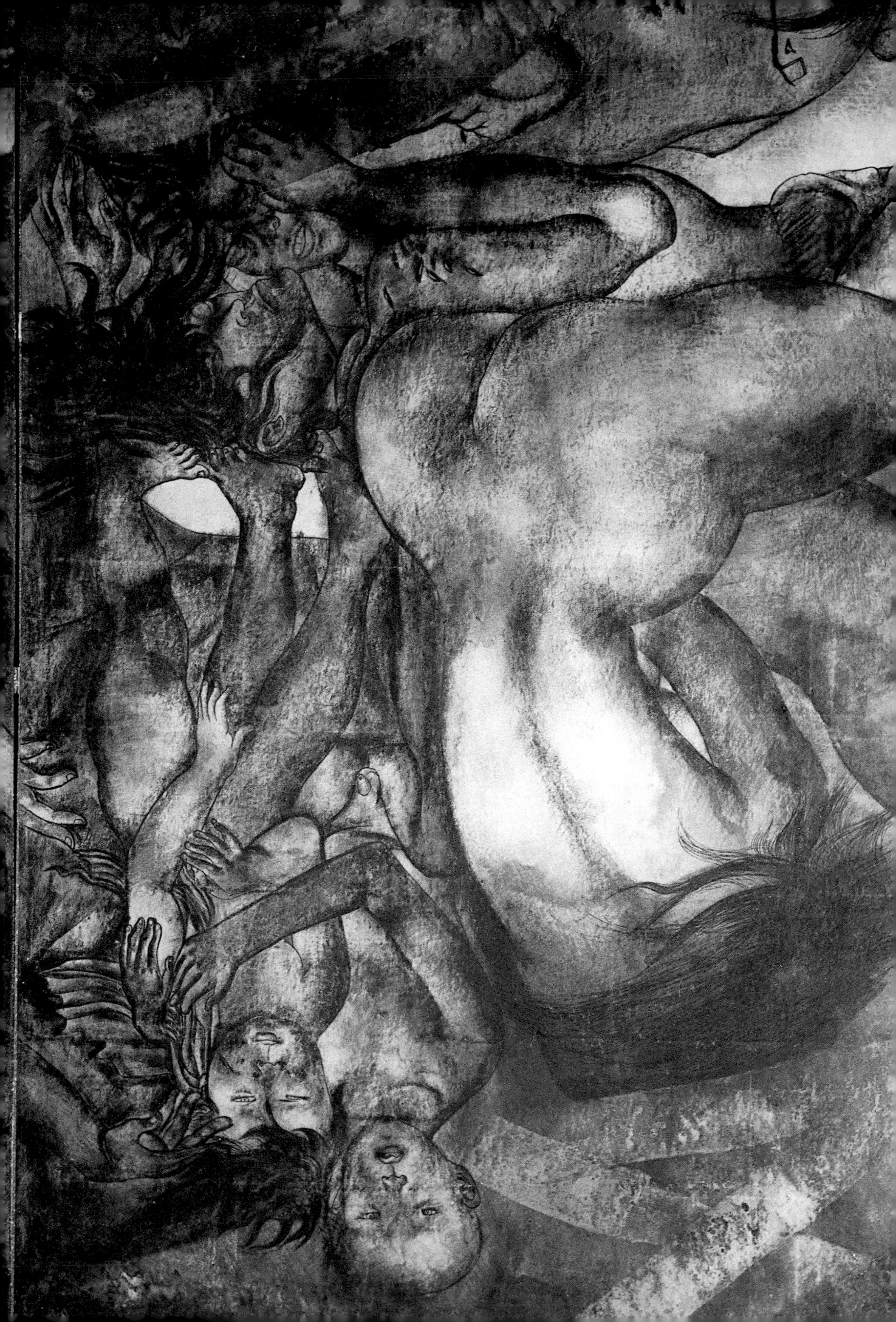

A few weeks later even those who were uninjured develop strange symptoms. At first there is nausea, vomiting, diarrhea, and then purple spots erupting under the skin. Blood issues from their gums, throat, rectum, and urinary tract. Their hair begins to fall out. Their white blood cell count drops. For many there will be gradual weakening until death.

At this time the *hibakusha* do not know they are suffering from radiation effects. They only know that they, like their city, have experienced some terrible holocaust.

Because census and military records were destroyed, no one can fully count the dead. Estimates go as high as two hundred thousand, or more.

You recall that the atomic bomb that obliterated Hiroshima was nicknamed *The Little Boy*—that it was, indeed, a small child compared to the thermonuclear giants that have sprung up since then.

There was the rumor that trees and flowers would never grow again in Hiroshima. That everyone who had been exposed to the bomb would be dead within three years. That for seventy-five years no one could live there.

Trees and flowers are blooming again, as if Nature herself wants to forget this unnatural catastrophe. But you know that should a nuclear war break out today, even Nature will not be able to forget.

The Aioi Bridge, which was the target site of the Enola Gay, once more spans the Ota River where pleasure boats, instead of corpses, are carried along by the tide. Only the *hibakusha* notice that the water seems darker since that day so many sought refuge there and drowned.

Once again everyone comes to picnic under the cherry trees that line the shore. It doesn't seem to matter that the trees, like most of their admirers, took root here after the war.

Hiroshima is now officially called The City of Peace. But for the *hibakusha* the atomic mushroom still hangs in the sky.

Visit the Atomic Dome in the Peace Park.

This ghostly structure has become the symbol of Hiroshima's fate. Originally it was the Industrial Exhibition Hall, designed by an Austrian architect to display the prefectural wares. Now it displays the destructive power of the world's first nuclear weapon.

Over the years the dome was the center of controversy. There were those who demanded that it be torn down so that Hiroshima could forget its scars and become like any other place. Others insisted it should remain as a warning to the rest of the world. And a third group, with Asian resignation, suggested letting it stand until it fell naturally of its own force.

The local government finally resolved the issue. The Atomic Dome is to be preserved. Its wounded presence shall continue to preside over the city.

Stroll through the Peace Park.

In some ways it might be a park anywhere, but it was laid out in the early fifties to mark the hypocenter of the explosion. People wander through it casually; little ones frolic in the grass and feed the pigeons; old men sit in the sun.

However, bus loads of children are brought in regularly from all parts of the country on school tours. As if there is a lesson to be learned here.

You realize that the young, too, are tourists in this place. August 6, 1945 is a long time ago—long before they were born.

Pause at the Cenotaph.

Beneath this graceful replica of an ancient clay house lies the registry of those who perished from the bomb. As *hibakusha* die over the years, their names are added to the sacred list.

You watch people come up and lay flowers or light incense here. This hallowed spot where the souls of the dead are believed to reside draws you into its sorrow. For that moment you peer deep into the abyss created by an atomic explosion. And you realize that you, too, are a survivor.

The plaque on the repository of names reads: "Rest in peace. The mistake will not be repeated."

You wonder—like so many Japanese have wondered—whose mistake?

And—like the rest of the world—you wonder: Will it be repeated?

供
世界連邦建設同盟
新居浜支部
代表 越智慎一
真鍋梅一
敬

Stop by the Memorial Mound for the Unknown Dead.

Tens of thousands of boxes of ashes, most of them unidentified, lay in the vault below waiting to be claimed by relatives. As remains of bomb victims are discovered even now in excavation sites, they are cremated and stored with the others.

Those who were never able to locate their loved ones and give them a proper burial offer special prayers to placate the souls of the homeless dead.

Look at the Children's Monument.

It was erected in 1958 in memory of Sadako Sasaki, the Anne Frank of Hiroshima. Her death from delayed radiation effects, ten years after the bomb fell, was to symbolize what a bomb did to the first children who experienced it.

Sadako was almost two when the bomb exploded a mile from her home, hurling her from the breakfast table across the room. Seemingly unharmed, she fled with her mother and older brother to the Ota River where they found space on a small boat anchored in the middle, and were drenched by the radioactive black rain that fell intermittently through the day.

Until the age of twelve, Sadako appeared to be a normal, healthy girl. She was the best runner in her sixth grade class when she suddenly developed the symptoms of leukemia.

According to the legend that has grown up around her, Sadako was very brave in the hospital. "I don't want to die," she confided to her mother, but she managed to laugh and sing gaily when her classmates came to visit her. Secretly she kept a chart of her daily white blood cell count under her mattress. And she folded paper cranes.

There is an old belief in Japan that a crane can live for a thousand years. If you fold a thousand paper cranes, they will protect you from illness. But Sadako did not have the strength or time to reach a thousand. On October 25, 1955, when she had made only nine hundred sixty four, she died. Her friends added the missing cranes and placed them in the coffin with her.

And then with the zeal of crusaders, Sadako's class started a national school campaign to build a monument to her, which would honor all children who had suffered from the bomb.

It is a powerful memorial. On the top of an oval granite pedestal, which symbolizes Mt. Horai, the fabled mountain of paradise, a young girl stands holding a golden crane in her outstretched arms. Inside the pedestal is space for the colorful paper crane leis that children and adults have been sending from all over Japan and abroad.

At the base are the words: "This is our cry, this is our prayer: Peace in the world!"

Go to the Peace Museum.

Let the pitiful testimony of inanimate objects—rock, metal, tile, stones, glass—twisted by the malevolent heat into grotesque shapes—tell their own story of this human-made disaster.

Many of these relics were gathered right from the burning ruins by a geologist who understood the historical importance of their bizarre configurations. While others searched through the rubble for pots, knives, and any other household items they might sell for survival, he collected his weird assortment of melted stones, roof tiles, and crockery to expose the "essence" of an atomic bomb's destructiveness.

The geologist even collected shadows, like the one of the man who sought refuge on the steps of the Sumitomo Bank. His body, vaporized by the heat and light of the bomb's explosion, was imprinted there as if he were being photographed for posterity.

The steps have been preserved as a reminder—after a nuclear blast, only the shadow of man remains, a shadow in the stone.

Walk through the museum.

The director tells you that a million people pass through each year. He has placed scientific graphs and data about nuclear radioactivity among the exhibits in order to "educate" rather than "shock" the viewers.

You wonder: Should anyone be protected from the shock of the bomb? Isn't everyone already too protected from the true horror of a nuclear weapon?

You walk past the disintegrated remains of school uniforms worn by some of the six thousand children who had been mobilized with their teachers to tear down houses in the center of the city for fire lanes.

Those not killed instantly by the intense radiation of the blast were charred beyond recognition and died by nightfall.

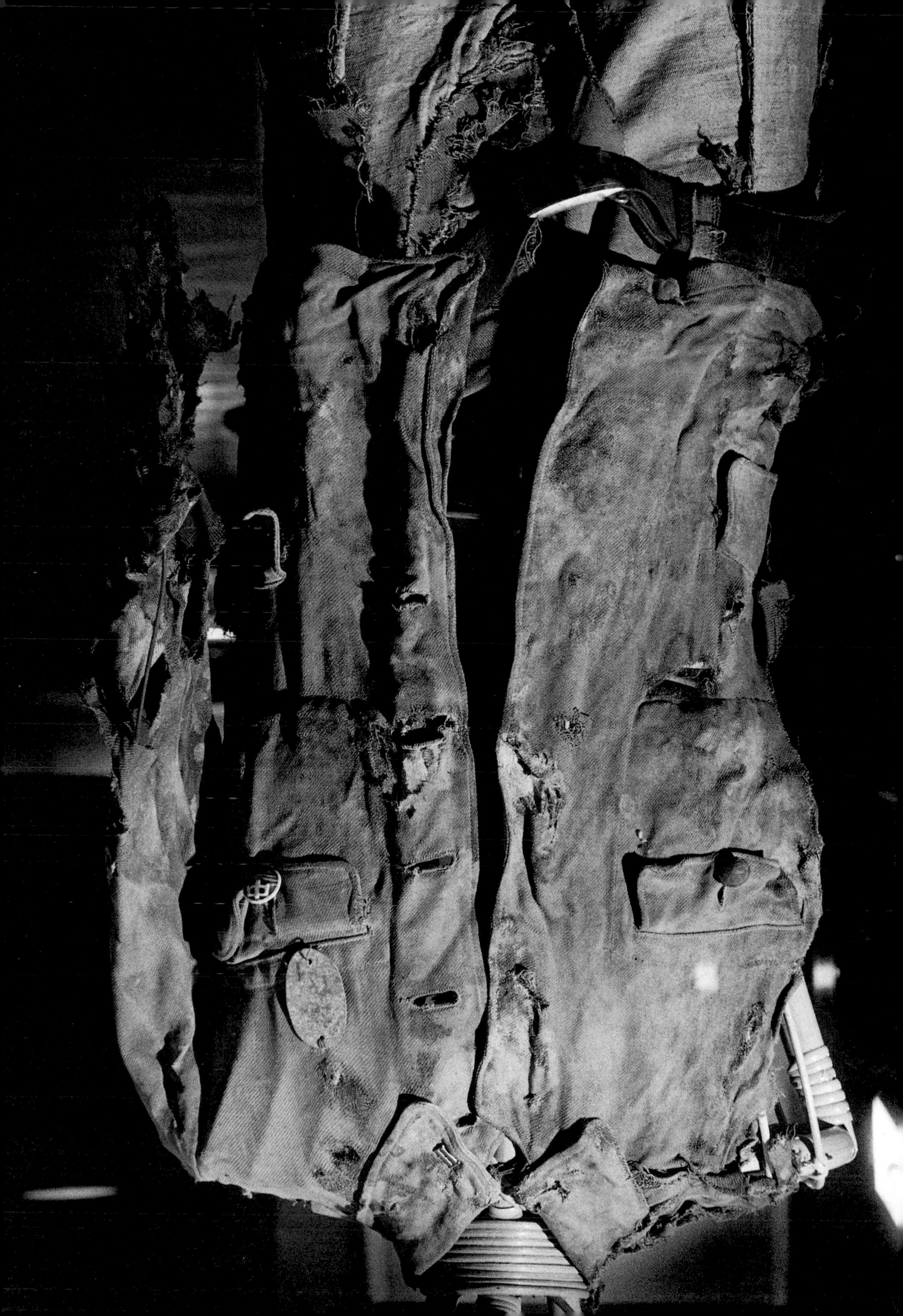

You pause before one life-size mannequin in this macabre fashion show and feel compelled to trace her identity, know her story.

Her name was Ryoko Hatsuya.

She was thirty-three, a gentle person who loved poetry, her husband tells you. On that morning of August 6 she had joined a women's brigade clearing fire lanes behind City Hall. She felt something like a million flash bulbs exploding in her face and passed out. When she regained consciousness sometime later, she groped along a railroad track, the one familiar path in the unfamiliar wilderness, to find her way home.

Her husband made a little tent for her in the back of what

remained of the soy sauce factory he had managed. The skin was hanging from her swollen face and the upper part of her body was severely burned, but he had only cooking oil and flour to put on her wounds.

Ryoko's mother-in-law came as fast as she could from Tokyo when she heard that Hiroshima had been annihilated. She hoped to find the bones of her son and his wife to carry back to the ancestral grave. She could hardly believe that they were alive.

But she came too late. Ryoko's hair was falling out, she had diarrhea and vomiting. When she saw her mother-in-law, she wanted to be held like a baby. She died three days later. Her last words were an apology that she had not given her husband a child.

Ryoko's mother-in-law was a strong woman, but she was overwhelmed by the suffering she witnessed in Hiroshima. She decided to purify herself by living for three years in a cave on the mountaintop of the nearby holy island of Miyajima.

"I prayed for Ryoko and for the world," she said. "I hoped that when I returned to Hiroshima, I would have special powers to help the *hibakusha*."

She became a Shinto priestess, known as the *Yama-no-Obaasan*, the old woman of the mountain, to those who sought her out in pain and despair. Armed with special herbs and spiritual power, she spent the rest of her life trying to defeat the dark power of the bomb.

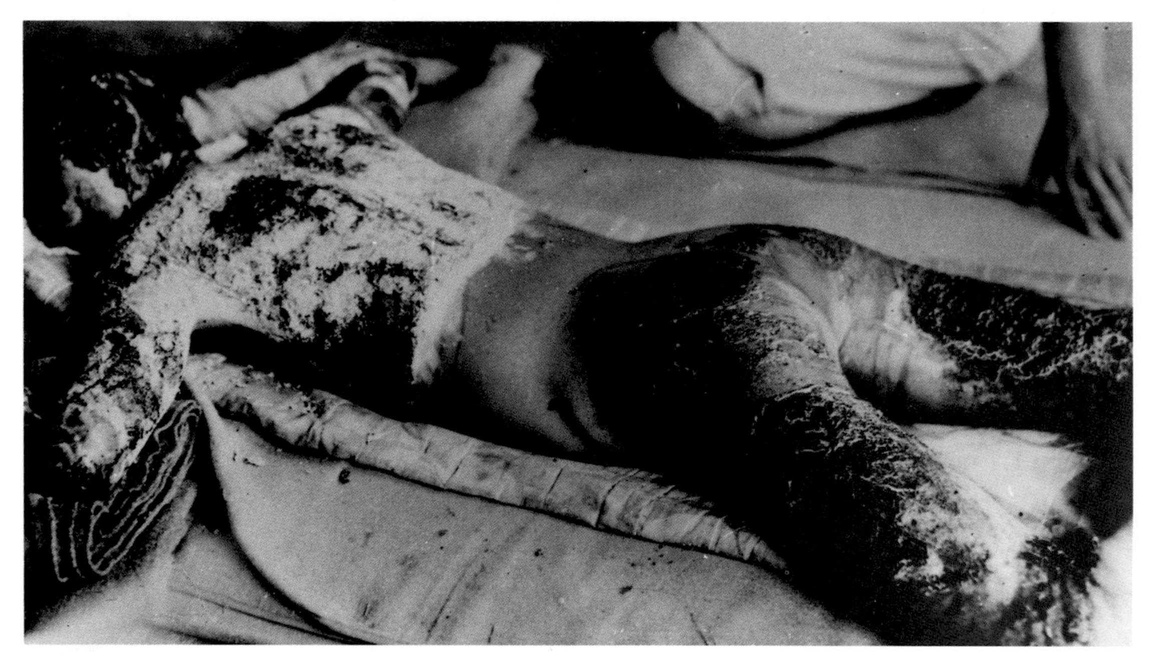

Photographs tell, as nothing else can, the destructive power of that first small bomb.

You walk with others in silence past the wounded victims stretched out in misery in makeshift first aid stations that had no adequate medical personnel or provisions to relieve the suffering.

You wonder what medical supplies would be available to victims of the nuclear arsenals that are being assembled today.

Would there be even one doctor left to dispense them?

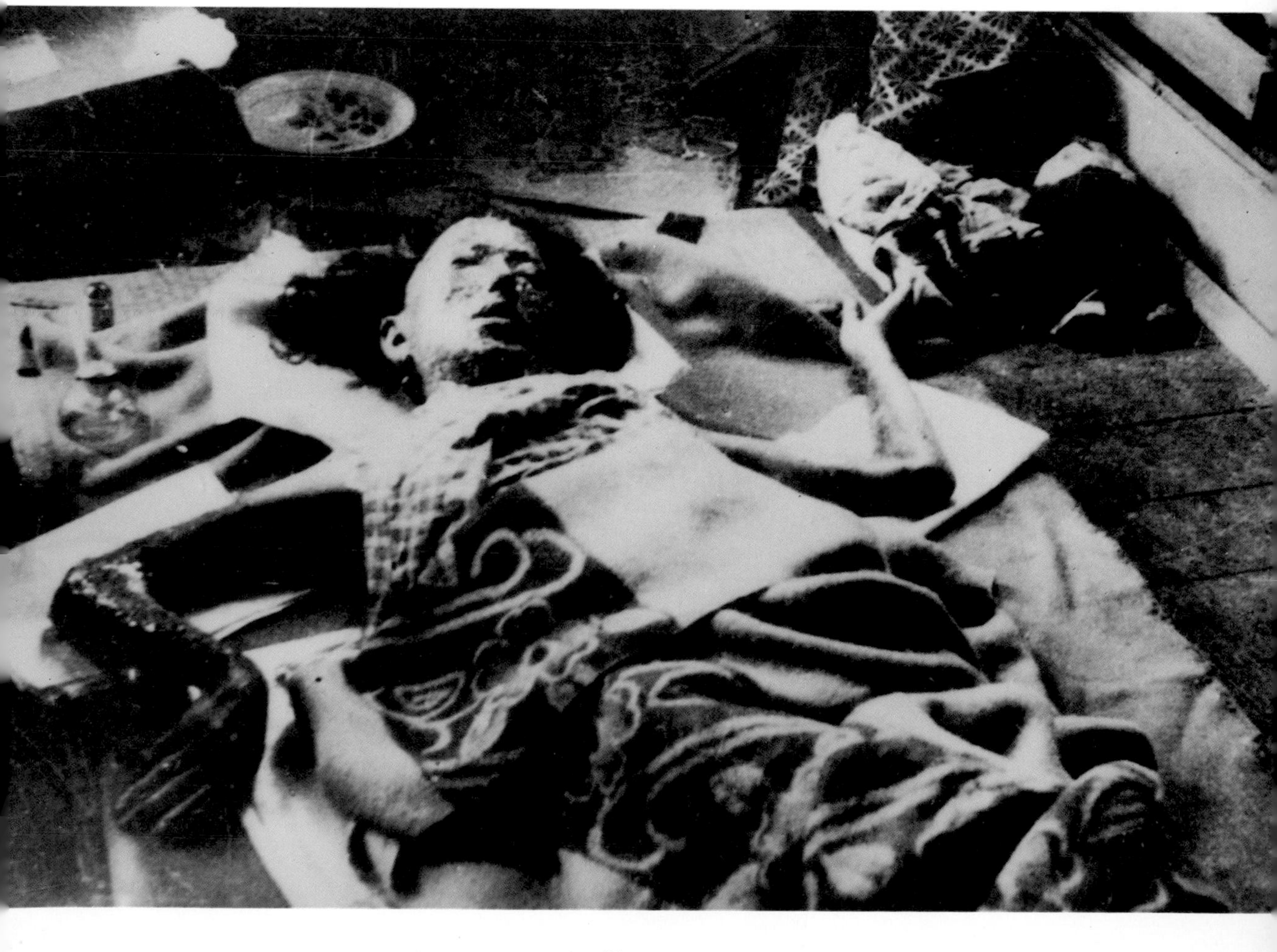

You learn that at least one of the badly wounded in those photographs did not die.

One day Tsuyako Wataji walked into the museum for the first time and recognized herself among the wounded in a high school gymnasium by the pattern in the kimono she was wearing that day. By then she was married and ran a gas station with her husband.

"It is terrible to recall that time," she tells you. "I was twenty-two, engaged to be married. I had volunteered to take my mother's place in the women's labor corps in the center of town. I remember dropping my lunch box off at my sister's house on the way, and looking at myself in the mirror as I left."

When she managed to return a short time later, a charred figure in scorched clothes, her sister did not recognize her. Somehow they got to the country house where the family had decided to meet in case of emergency.

"If you could come this far, you can live," her mother told her as she collapsed at the door. "I won't let you die from these burns."

When the army set up a dispensary at the local high school, her family took her there on a stretcher, and stayed with her, bringing fresh grapes from the vineyard, sometimes milk and eggs. She could hear the flies buzzing over the festering wounds of others who had no relatives to attend them. They defecated, vomited, and died right where they lay.

In a few months she grew stronger, but her face was so disfigured few people could bear to look at her. When her fiancé got a job in Tokyo, she refused to marry him because she was ashamed to be seen by outsiders.

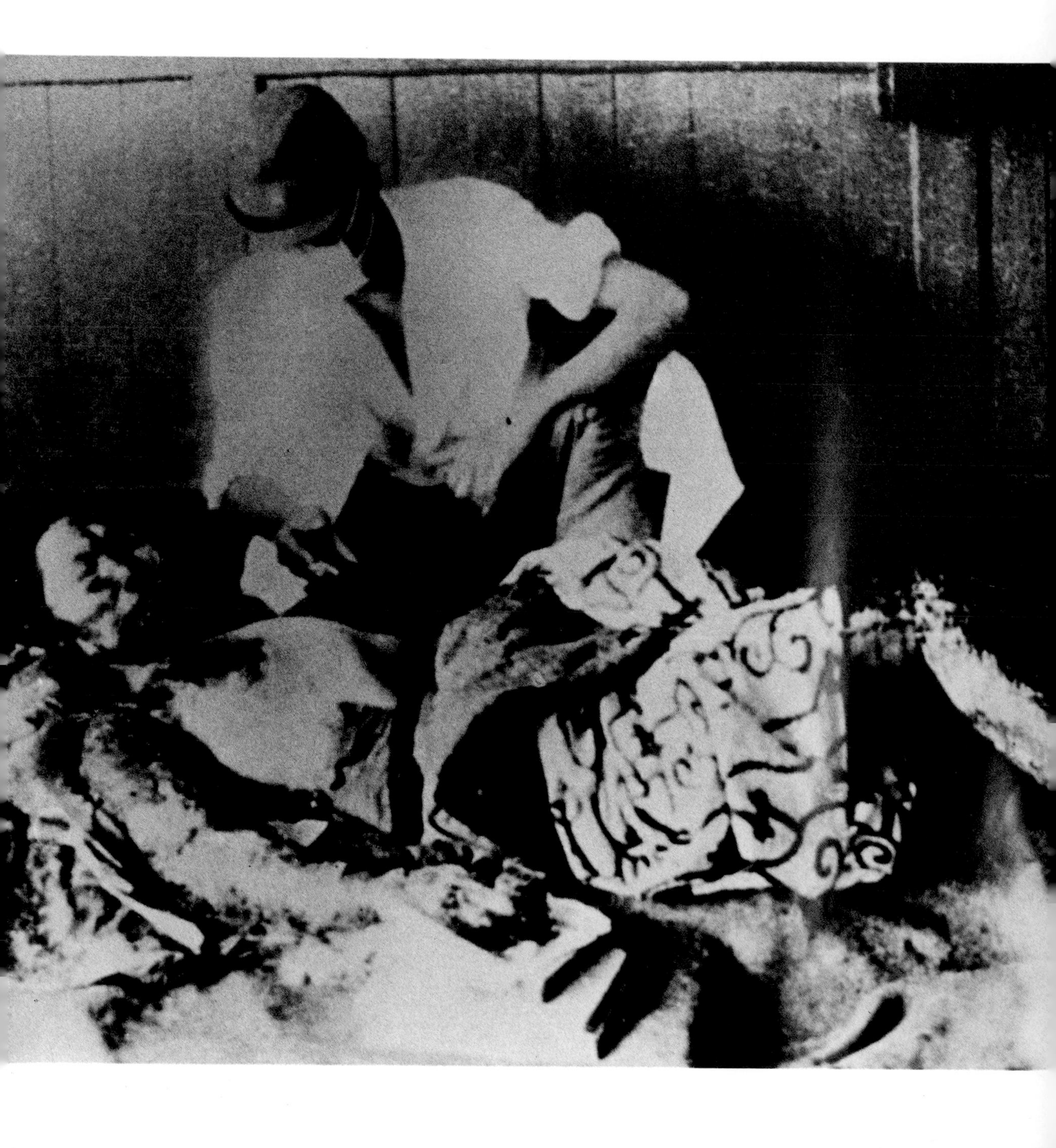

Eventually she did marry a childhood friend because she was able to feel comfortable with him in the isolation of their farm. But the work proved too much: in the winter her hands would swell, in the summer her skin could not tolerate sunlight. Moving back into town with their three children, she and her husband opened the gas station.

Except for occasional fatigue, she feels fine now. But dark reddish spots have appeared under her eyes, which her doctor is unable to explain.

"I just go on with my life day by day at the station," she says. "I try not to worry that my children will come down with anything or that their children won't be normal. Compared to other survivors, I know I am lucky."

CALTEX
GS
バッテリー

Now you understand that the survivors of Hiroshima are different from people who survive conventional bombing. They may look like everyone else, but they harbor a deep fear that the invisible contamination lodged in their bodies might erupt at any moment into what has come to be known as A-Bomb disease.

For the medical profession, A-Bomb disease is any illness that can be proven to be caused by radiation effects on the body. Leukemia and thyroid and breast cancer appeared in disproportionate numbers in the first decades after the war. Now stomach,

lung, and uterine cancer is on the increase, as well as cataracts, liver and blood diseases, heart and kidney disturbances, and endocrine and skin disorders.

For the fearful survivors, A-Bomb disease is any illness that afflicts them, whether medically verified or not. They suffer a number of mysterious ailments, the most common being bouts of weakness, for which there is no clear cause or cure. What is clear is that A-Bomb disease has become as much an emotional disease as a physical one. There is never an end to anxiety.

Go to the A-Bomb Hospital.

Since it was completed in 1956, its one hundred and seventy beds have always been filled with officially recognized *hibakusha*. To be eligible for free treatment here, one has to have been within the city limits at the time of the blast, have come into the center of the city to find relatives or do rescue work during the following two weeks, or have been exposed in utero.

For many survivors who check in and out of the hospital with severe chronic ailments, the A-Bomb Hospital has become a second home.

The late Dr. Fumio Shigeto, who served as director of the hospital for many years, was himself a survivor.

"It is getting difficult to tell who is suffering from A-Bomb disease and who from the natural process of aging," he once told you. But he was careful to add, "I think it is both."

For all doctors here try to weigh their words carefully; they know that these old survivors, who were the first in the world to experience a nuclear attack, have been exposed to tremendous doses of radiation. The aging process appears to have accelerated in them, with a larger number suffering from heart disease, malignant tumors, and arteriosclerosis than in unexposed elderly patients.

But Dr. Shigeto did not get involved in scientific disputations. "My job is to decrease the pain of my patients," he would say. "To make them feel glad they lived, rather than sorry."

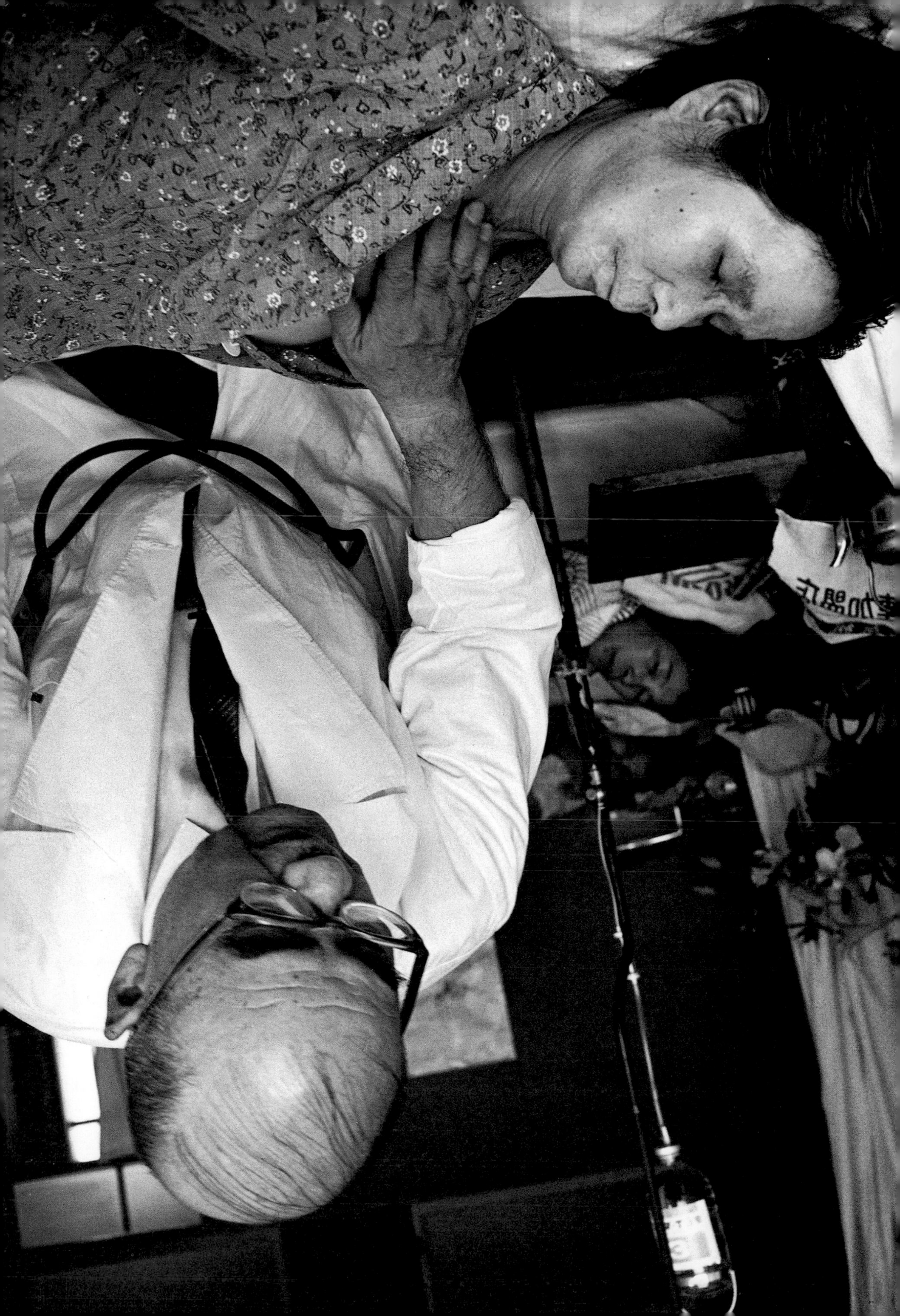

You remember one of the first patients you met—Shigeo Taguchi who had been in and out of the hospital for a series of elbow operations.

"I used to hate Americans," he felt the need to inform you.

All of his family died from radiation effects a few months after the bomb fell. His eyesight damaged, his arm useless, he drank heavily and carried a knife, hoping to kill an American. It was a girlfriend who took the knife away from him, advising him to plan his life, rather than remaining stuck in the past.

Now married, with three children, Taguchi not only was leading a boy scout troop, but had arranged for it to exchange letters with an American troop. He held a job as a clerk in a big rayon company.

"But don't get the idea my life is successful," he warned you. "A survivor is one step behind other people in promotion because he has to take so many medical leaves—like this one."

Then Taguchi related a story about the day of the bomb that he'd always dreamed of telling an American.

"I was twenty-three, home on leave," he began. "I could hardly wait for August 6 because I was invited to the birthday party of the beautiful girl next door whom I'd always been too shy to talk to."

"On that morning I woke early and went outside hoping to catch a glimpse of her. Instead I saw something that looked like a pink ball falling through the sky. I thought some B-29 had dropped a flare by mistake. Suddenly it got dark. The next thing I knew, I was pinned under my house."

"My mother rescued me, and managed to get to my sisters. As we fled through our garden from the fires that were breaking out all around us, I saw that the girl next door was pinned under a beam of her house. I ran to help her mother who was desperately trying to pull her out."

"The girl was still conscious and begged her mother and me to escape the flames that were by now almost on top of us. We fled into the black rain that was pouring down over the city."

"I didn't come back to the ruins of our house until much later. I saw the charred bones of the girl next door where we had left her. Her mother was standing there in bewilderment. She kept talking about the birthday party we were supposed to have on August 6."

Marie Nishido, a former nurse, has been in and out of the hospital for years suffering from pernicious anemia.

She wasn't hurt when her boarding house, a mile from the hypocenter, collapsed. She spent the next month caring for the wounded in a hospital until she too came down with radiation illness.

"My hair fell out and my gums bled, but I recovered," she said that first time you visited her. "For the next seventeen years I was fine. I married a farmer and had two children when I suddenly started getting dizzy and needing blood transfusions."

Sometimes it seemed that the psychological stress of being separated from her two children during her hospital sojourns was worse than the anemia. Her doctors warned her that she would never recover if she didn't stop brooding about them.

Commuting now from her farm for weekly blood transfusions, Mrs. Nishido believes that it was only the desire to be reunited with her children that kept her alive. "But every time I hear of nuclear testing somewhere in the world, I feel weak," she says. "If mothers in other countries knew the misery of being separated from their children, they would cry out for peace."

Like many other *hibakusha*, who until now have been locked in their own private agony, Mrs. Nishido is getting the courage to cry out so that all of her suffering will not have been in vain.

As sixty-year-old Sugie Ota endeavors to talk to you, her sightless eyes stare up in the fixed position they have had ever since that day they happened to look up at a bright light exploding in the sky.

She was seven months pregnant and opening a window in the entrance of her house. The next thing she knew her body felt like it was on fire, and she was running with her bleeding three-year-old son to a clinic in the neighborhood school. She was blind, severely burned, and unconscious when relatives took her and the child to their country home where her husband, who had been injured by shattered glass while having his hair cut, was waiting. Her baby was born twelve days later. It cried once, and died. Her son died three weeks after that.

There was nothing to put on her festering burns but vegetable oil. Some of the victims in the area had found that ashes acted like powder on a wound, and that those of loved ones just being cremated were especially beneficial. And so her family ground the bones of her dead children into a fine powder and applied it to her face. Although her arms would remain badly scarred, Mrs. Ota thanks the ashes of her children for the fact that her face did not have a blemish when it healed.

She managed to give birth to yet another son two years later and to breast feed him. But although she was in and out of hospitals having skin grafts on both arms, nothing could restore the muscles in her hands, which remain permanently crippled.

Now widowed—her husband died of throat cancer ten years before—Mrs. Ota is completely immobilized with rheumatism and arthritis. She is not bitter. "It was war," she says, "and couldn't be helped." She enjoys listening to television, even though she can't see it, and feels sustained by the Shinso sect of Buddhism. She and her husband often visited shrines, giving thanks that they were alive.

If she had a message for the world, what would it be? you ask her.

"Don't test nuclear bombs, ban them," she says.

And then she sits there in silence, as if there is nothing more to say.

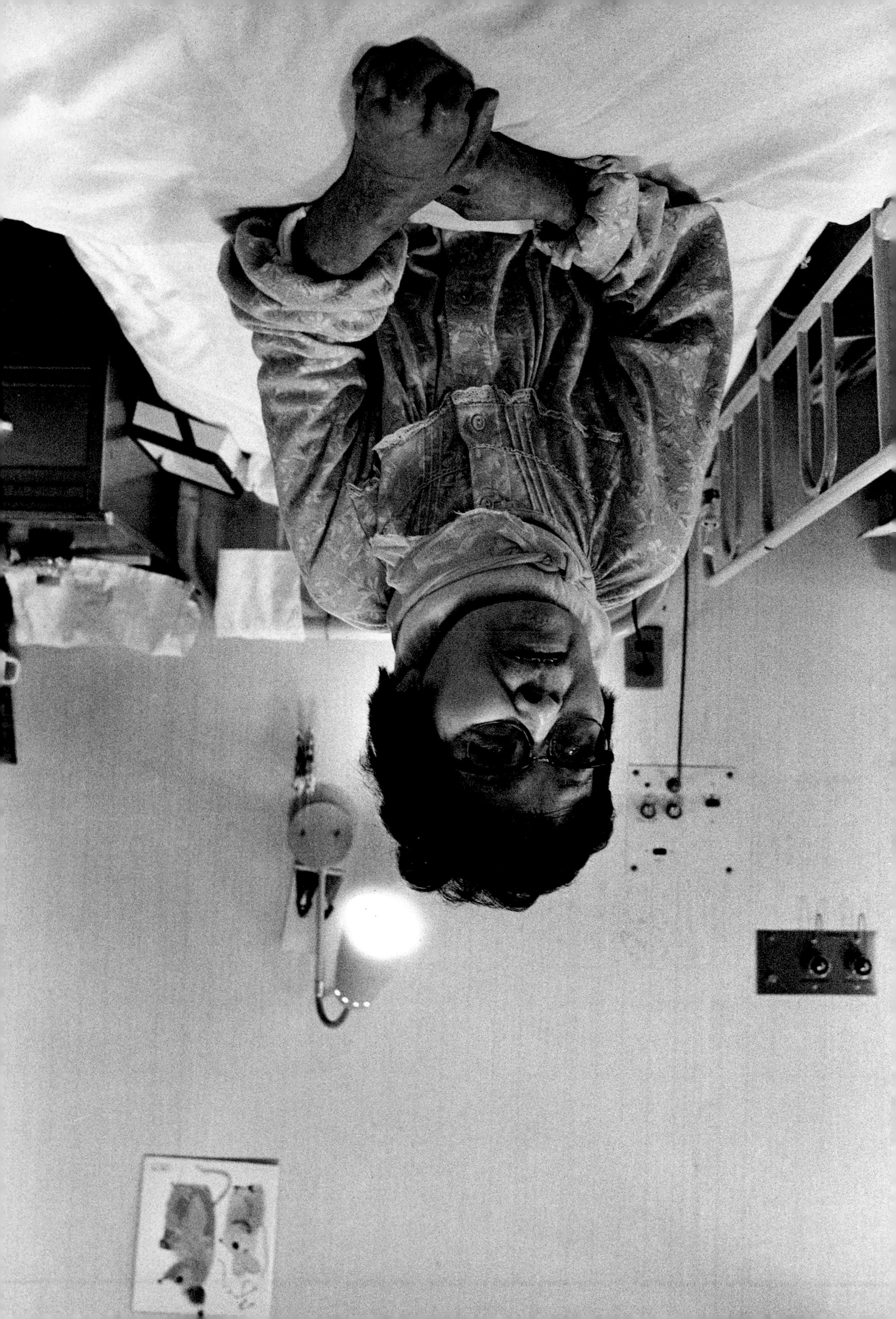

What happened to the babies who didn't die at birth, like Mrs. Ota's—who were exposed in utero and lived?

You learn that children whose mothers were three or four months pregnant and within two miles of the hypocenter were prone to disorders of the central nervous system. Many of them died within the first year. Others were born microcephalic—with small heads and mental retardation.

The families of the microcephalic children struggled to raise them without medical assistance in depressed areas known as "atomic slums," not realizing that their children's condition was related to the bomb. The slums have been replaced with high rise apartments, but the mentality of the children has not increased.

Upon discovering each other's existence, twenty-four families organized The Mushroom Club, whose name refers both to the mushroom shape of the cloud, and the fact that these children are growing like mushrooms in the shade. They suffer from various disorders such as eye problems, hip dislocation, epileptic fits, high blood pressure, kidney and liver diseases. An unknown number have already died.

The Mushroom Club members have demanded and received government support, but not enough to compensate for what their children would have earned were they normal. One of the club's main concerns is what will happen to these children when their parents die.

Yuriko Hatanaka is middle-aged, and still not toilet trained. She understands only the simplest things, and speaks in shrill gutteral tones. Not being able to handle chopsticks, she eats with her fingers.

Yuriko's mother was three months pregnant when she went with a small child on her back to help serve food for a women's group dismantling buildings in the center of the city. Her child was killed outright, as were most of the women workers. Despite acute radiation sickness, she survived and delivered a seemingly normal baby in February of 1946.

It wasn't until Yuriko was four that her parents noticed her strange walk. She was diagnosed a microcephalic by a doctor from Hiroshima Medical School. From that time on she stayed in the family barbershop with her mother and father, or played with the small children in the neighborhood.

Yuriko seems to know that her mother died last year. When allowed to hold the jar with her mother's ashes, she placed it next to her ear, as if hoping to hear her mother's voice.

Now she sits forlorn with her father in the barbershop during the day. Her younger sister, who is married and lives next door, has taken full charge of dressing and feeding her like another one of her babies.

You realize that nuclear weapons have given us the power to destroy our own species.

What of those who were small children when the bomb fell?

They can remember nothing—but neither can they forget. It could be said that they grew up with the bomb. They know that radiation waits like a time bomb within the human body—that it could be waiting in theirs.

Watching Yuki Muneoka play with her nursery school classes over the years, it was hard to believe she had a care in the world. Like Sadako Sasaki, she was two when the bomb fell a mile from her home, and uninjured. Her father was wounded in the post office and died a year later. One of her sisters was never found.

In the third grade of high school, she began suffering from acute anemia. For the next four years she was in and out of hospitals. Now she receives periodic blood transfusions.

Yuki believed that no one would marry her. "Japanese consider survivors tainted," she would say. "They want women in the family who will produce healthy children."

But Yuki did marry and move away. Address unknown.

You wonder if her husband knows that she is a survivor, or if she is passing in some new city.

You wonder if she is well.

What became of the thousands of children who were orphaned on that August 6?

Many of them were raised just across from Hiroshima on the tiny island of Ninoshima, otherwise known as Boy's Island.

The orphanage was founded in the fall of 1946 by an idealistic school teacher, Yoshimaru Mori, who was troubled by the hordes of vagrant children hanging around the railroad station, taking part in black marketeering and prostitution. He felt that the island, which had once been a quarantine station for the Imperial Navy, would be the best place for these homeless waifs.

One night he went out with a truck and literally abducted sixty orphans at the station. He took off at high speed for the pier. When he got there, he had only forty-three boys left, but they were the original ones to come to Boy's Island.

Only one of the original war orphans remains as a teacher on the island. Yoshiki Yamanouchi was ten when he arrived with scars over half of his body. His widowed mother was killed on her way to work in the building that is now the Atomic Dome. He and his younger brother pulled their sister from the wreckage of their house, but in the confusion of those chaotic weeks, they became separated and found each other only thirty years later.

Yamanouchi is not sure just why he remains on Boy's Island. Perhaps it is ties of the past that hold him, he tells you. And the feeling that he wants to give something to these new children who are homeless, although for reasons other than his own.

Perhaps he doesn't feel tough enough to face the cruel realities in this family oriented society that discriminates against orphans, as well as survivors.

Perhaps he is ashamed of the thick overgrowth of scar tissue, known as keloids, from the Greek word for crab claws, that trails down the back of his neck. He tries to keep the keloids hidden whenever he goes to the mainland to listen to music, drink beer, and play *pachinko*, the popular pinball machine.

On the island he can forget he is a *hibakusha*. But sometimes, like when his sneaker irritates the jagged keloid over his ankle during a ball game, he can't help but remember.

What of the children who were born to survivors years after the bomb? They are known as *hibakusha nisei*, second generation survivors.

They could also be called children of the bomb.

Mami-chan was just a baby when her mother died of leukemia caused by delayed radiation effects seventeen years after the bomb fell.

From the time she could walk, Mami-chan, accompanied by her grandmother, carried her mother's deathbed picture in her arms, much as she carried the sorrow in her heart, to anti-war parades, to August 6 ceremonies, to any commemoration that was held for *hibakusha*.

You read Mami-chan's mother's hospital diary, which was published after her death under the title *A Crane Who Cannot Come Back*.

> JANUARY 29, 1957
>
> I cannot help but think of the future of Mami-chan. I want her to be a well educated person—even if she is only a girl. I do not want her to have an experience like mine. Oh, how I wish I could hold her in my arms all the time.
>
> FEBRUARY 22, 1958 (the last entry)
>
> Tears stream down ceaselessly. One more patient has died tonight. I don't want to die. Mami-chan, my only daughter! And I, her only mother! Oh, this feeling—this lonely feeling.

Mami-chan would grow up and go to college. She would marry and have two healthy children. It is as if her crane mother is still watching over her.

故瀬戸奈々子(27才)

You first met Yoko when she was nineteen, living with her *hibakusha* parents in two small straw matted rooms over a milk shop. She brought you home, but not her many boyfriends who did not know she was the child of survivors. You realize that second generation children like Yoko have internalized the stigma as well as the fear of the bomb which victimized their mothers and fathers.

Although confined to his bed with kidney, liver, and heart problems, Yoko's father proved to be a man of robust spirit.

"I feel I am twenty-five years old, because twenty-five years have passed since the bomb fell," he told you. "I died at that moment. And when I recovered a few months later from acute radiation symptoms, I felt as if I were reborn."

Being reborn was not easy. From the ruins of his house Yoko's father recovered only a *saké* bottle that had melted into a dish. He was to be hospitalized many times, and his wife, herself weak from kidney problems, was forced to take in sewing to pay the medical bills.

When you see Yoko again, her parents have both died in the A-Bomb Hospital.

She is married and lives in a low income housing project across from the castle. She has two children now, a boy of nine and a girl of five. Her husband has accepted her *hibakusha* background, but her in-laws have never mentioned it, as if avoiding the subject dispels its reality.

Yoko no longer has red highlights in her hair, and there is fatigue in her face. She is living for her children, she tells you. But she has not told them she is a second generation survivor, just as she has not told her friends in the housing project, who may or may not be keeping the same secret. She would like to live as if the bomb has no relationship to her life.

And yet—she was filled with anxiety when she came down with a mysterious ailment during her first pregnancy. Her son was weak at birth and has bronchial problems. Her daughter was born with epilepsy and has been on medication until this year.

Yoko has felt weak since her daughter's birth. She is frightened by the sharp pains she has had twice in her chest and hip. Her doctor attributes them to nerves.

"I feel very lonely," she tells you—a comment you have heard from other survivors who try to repress their most primal fears.

Kazuyoshi Yukawa had intestinal problems as a child and low blood pressure and liver problems as a young adult. Still it wasn't until his son was born mentally retarded nine years ago, that he understood what it was to be a *hibakusha nisei*.

Yukawa hears the usual response from most doctors that there is no positive evidence yet of intergenerational genetic damage from atomic bomb radiation. While not denying the possibility, they take the scientific position that it will take many generations to verify.

But Yukawa sees many of his *hibakusha nisei* friends having miscarriages and stillbirths, as well as retarded children like his own. And hearing them complain of weakness and physical ailments like his, he cannot help but believe that radiation effects are involved.

Yukawa met his wife at work, but only after their son was born did either of them learn that she too was a *hibakusha nisei*. Like so many survivors, her parents wanted to spare her the fear and taint that come with this sad knowledge. She hesitated to have another child, but their five-year-old daughter appears normal in spite of her frail constitution and unusually dry skin.

Overwhelmed by anxiety that they may be carrying invisible contamination, the Yukawas are now busy organizing other second generation survivors into a group that will pressure the government to conduct research and grant them the same free medical care that survivors have.

They don't want to hide—they want to face the truth.

祭
竹浦
清酒ホンシュウイチ
清酒ホン

Yukawa shows you a poem that he has written to his son Makoto—words that the boy will never be able to read:

Makoto, my beloved son—
People say you are a half wit,
    but I won't believe it.
Why should it be?
Because your mother and I
    are second generation survivors—

Listen, Makoto—
On August 6, 1945,
Your grandpa and grandma were hurt
    by the bomb,
but they kept wandering in the ashes
    looking for their lost daughter.
Two years later it took all of grandma's strength
    to bear me.
She lost her hearing and eyesight after that.
I was thinner than you are now, Makoto—
    always following a dragonfly
    with feverish intensity.
Grandpa would wipe the sweat from my brow
    with his bombed hands:
        "Die out, die out, fever of the A-Bomb!
        Die out, die out, fever of the bomb!"

Shiho is a *hibakusha sansei*—a third generation survivor—whose mother died of stomach cancer when she was six.

Shiho's grandmother was over two miles from the bomb's hypocenter, but she came into the city to search for relatives, and came down with A-Bomb disease. She was still ill when she gave birth to Shiho's mother in 1946.

Shiho is a dreamy child who insists on sleeping with her doting grandparents, who are raising her, although she has a room of her own. She has just joined the Folded Crane Club, which is dedicated to the remembrance of Sadako and all children killed by the bomb. She is aware that she is now in the same grade at the same school as Sadako was when she became ill. And her mother would have been Sadako's age had they both lived. Sometimes she takes the cranes that the club makes to school and reminds the class about Sadako. It makes her feel close to her mother.

Some men are meant to be the conscience of their time, and Ichiro Kawamoto who founded the Folded Crane Club in 1958 is one of them. From the time he came into the city to do rescue work shortly after the bomb fell, he has felt himself a witness.

Unable to bear the suffering of the children he saw dying of leukemia and other diseases over the years, Kawamoto guided Sadako's class in erecting a monument to her, and then formed the club, with his wife Tokie. Children of all ages gathered in their shack

located near Sadako's statue to fold cranes, visit survivors at the hospital, and write letters to heads of state pleading for universal disarmament.

As the people of Hiroshima became upwardly mobile along with the rest of Japan during the "prosperity boom" of the seventies, Kawamoto was one of the few who resisted change. He kept his job as a janitor in Jogakuin Girl's School so that he would have flexible hours for his club's activities.

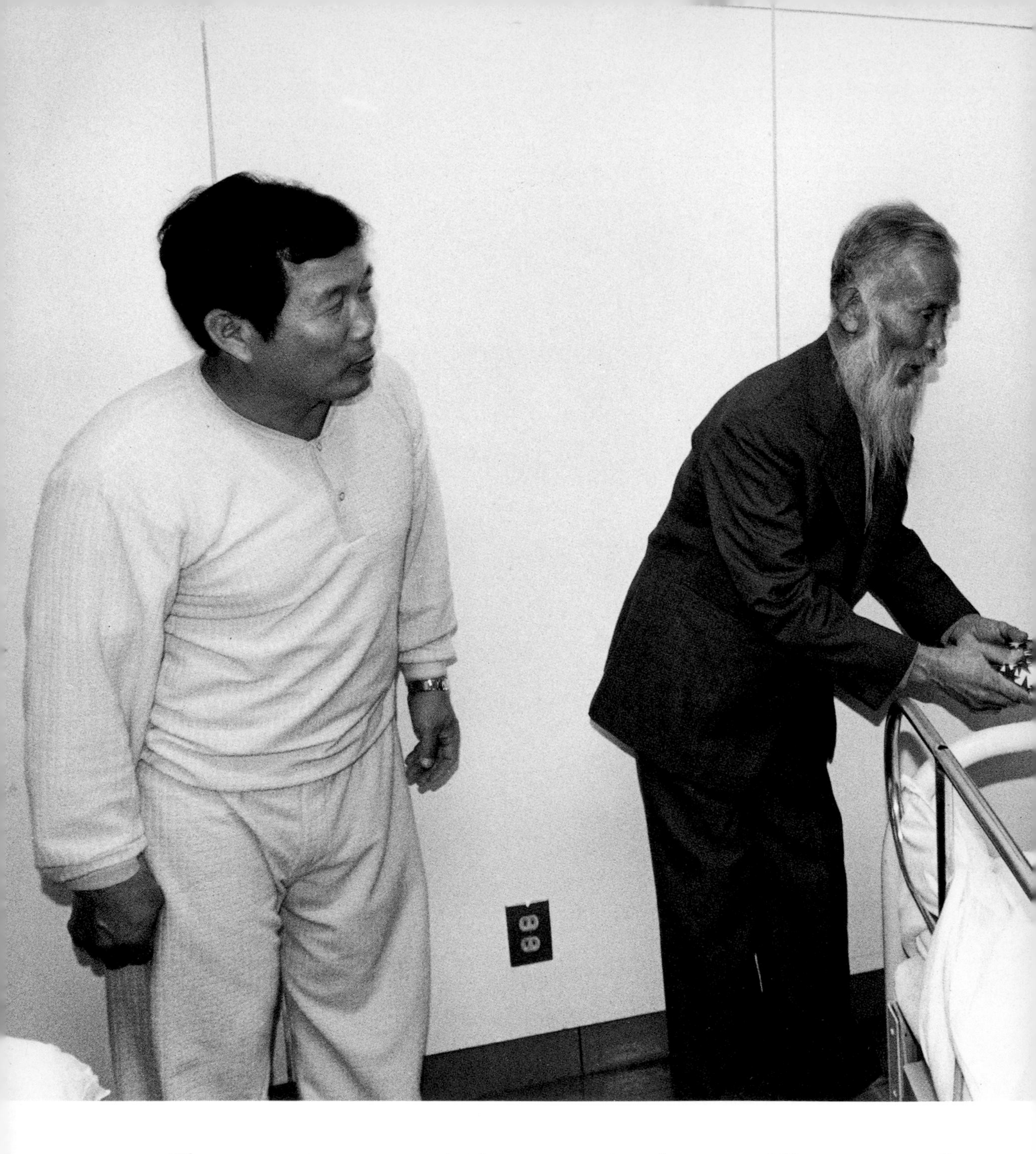

There were many parents in the community who accused Kawamoto and his wife of running a cult of the dead and steered their children toward more carefree activities. It was too hard a struggle. When his marriage fell apart, Kawamoto married a Korean *hibakusha*, one of eight thousand Koreans in Hiroshima during the war, to enable her to get medical privileges.

As a result of pressure from people like Kawamoto, the Japanese government has agreed to give free medical treatment, and the Korean government free round

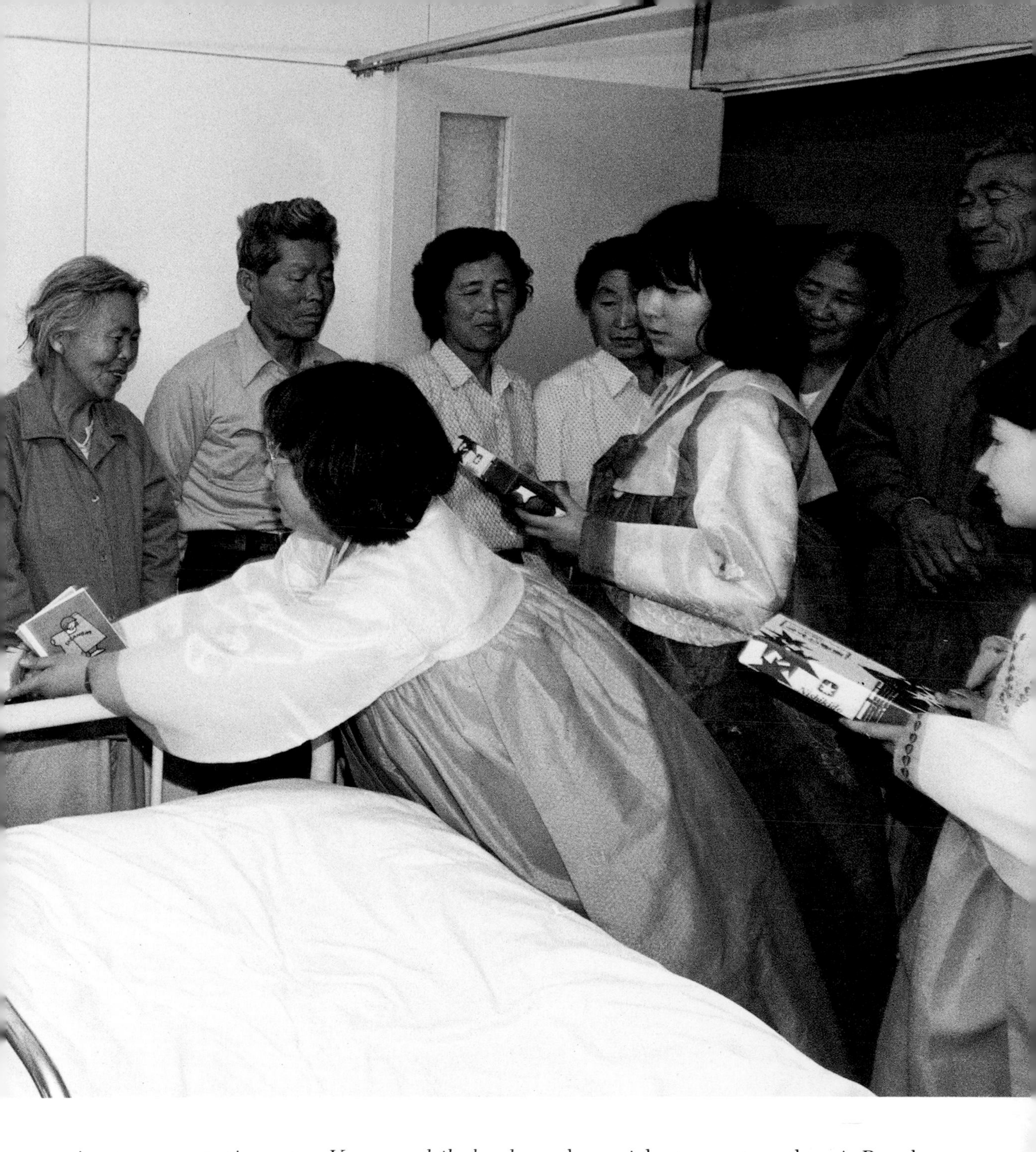

trip transportation, to Korean *hibakusha* who wish to enter the A-Bomb Hospital. Kawamoto encourages members of the Folded Crane Club, now mostly junior high school girls, to dress in Korean outfits when they visit the patients.

"I want our members to learn about this group of people that has met with so much discrimination," he says. "I want them to grow up without prejudice toward anyone. It is another way of working for peace in the world."

Hiroshima is filled with survivors who have never given up their personal struggle with the bomb. Kiyoshi Kikkawa was called A-Bomb Victim No. 1, but since his stroke several years ago he has been immobilized at a small hospital in the outskirts of the city.

A guard at the Hiroshima Electric Company a mile from the hypocenter, Kikkawa was badly burned on his arms and back. He managed to get home in time to rescue his wife from under their house, and the two of them spent the next five years at the Red Cross Hospital.

As his burns began to heal, massive bands of keloids formed grotesque patterns all over Kikkawa's back. Doctors displayed his scars to their colleagues, and then journalists discovered that here was a survivor who wanted them to witness the bomb's signature on human flesh.

Later Kikkawa would run a souvenir shop near the Atomic Dome, baring his back for Japanese and foreign tourists who requested a photograph. He was criticized by many for "selling the bomb," but in this period before the Memorial Museum, he felt it an educational duty to continue his one-man exhibit. He also helped establish the first association of A-Bomb victims that would call attention to the *hibakusha*'s terrible plight, as well as for an end to the nuclear arms race.

When his shack was torn down in 1963 to make room for the expansion of the Peace Park, Kikkawa opened a bar with his wife as hostess. It would become a meeting place for the sports and media world, and soon Kikkawa would be baring his back in *Hiroshima Mon Amour* and other films.

Kikkawa's dream to attend the UN's First Special Assembly for Disarmament in 1978 was thwarted by his stroke.

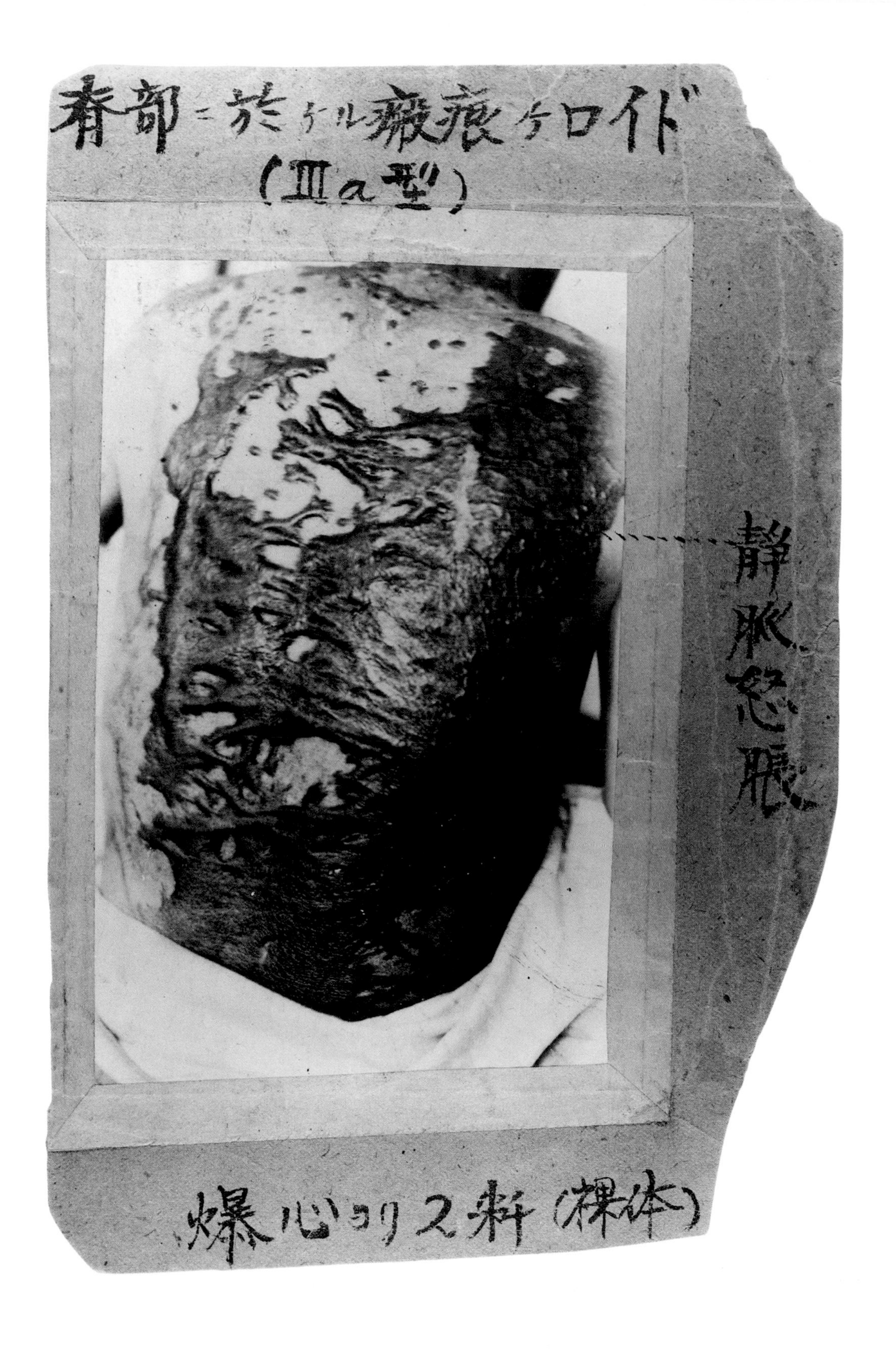

脊部ニ於ケル瘢痕ケロイド
(IIIa型)
静脈怒張
爆心ヨリ2粁(裸体)

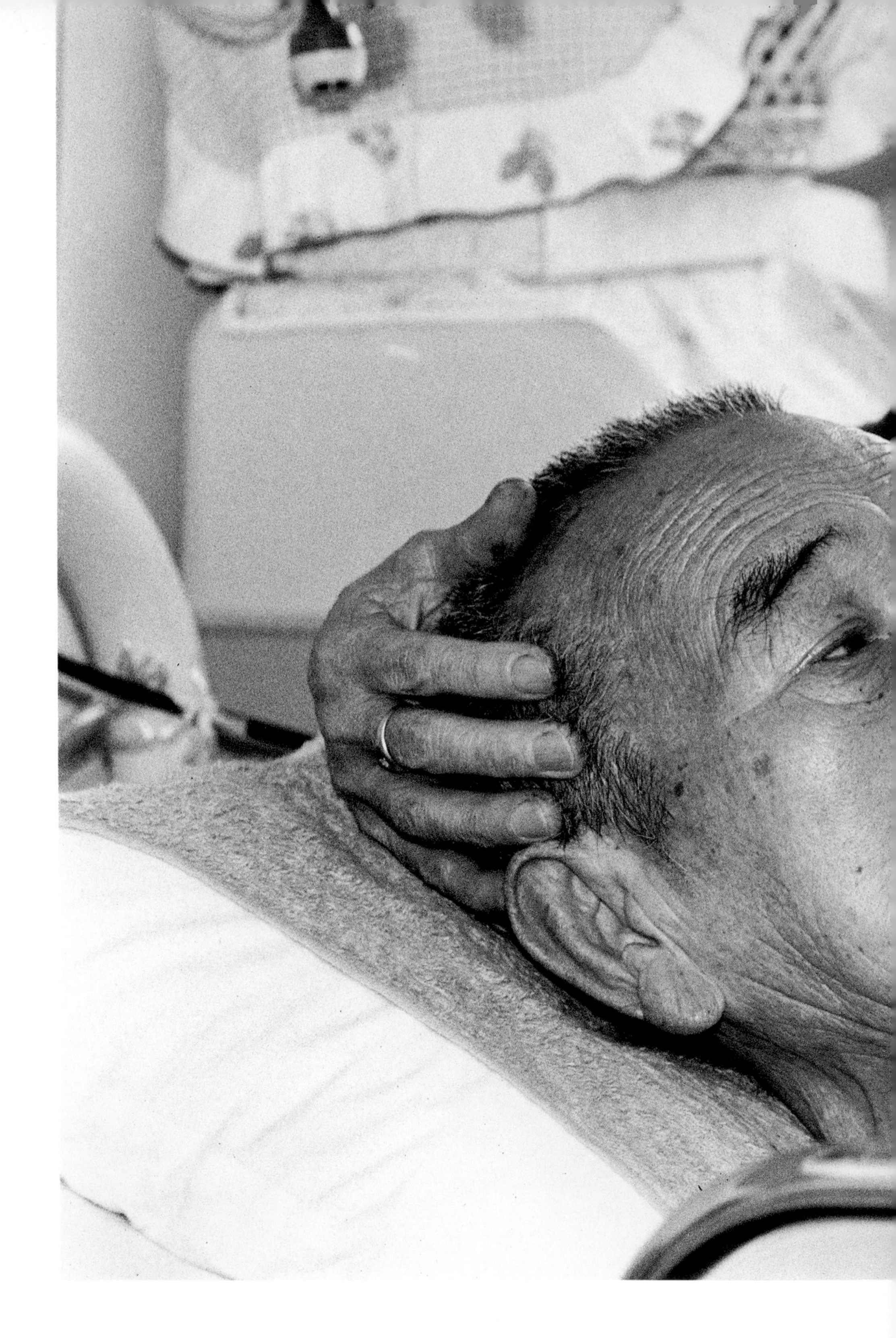

"What is the most important thing you have done in your life?" you ask Kikkawa, as he lies still paralyzed in his hospital bed six years later.

"Everything I have done is important," he says.

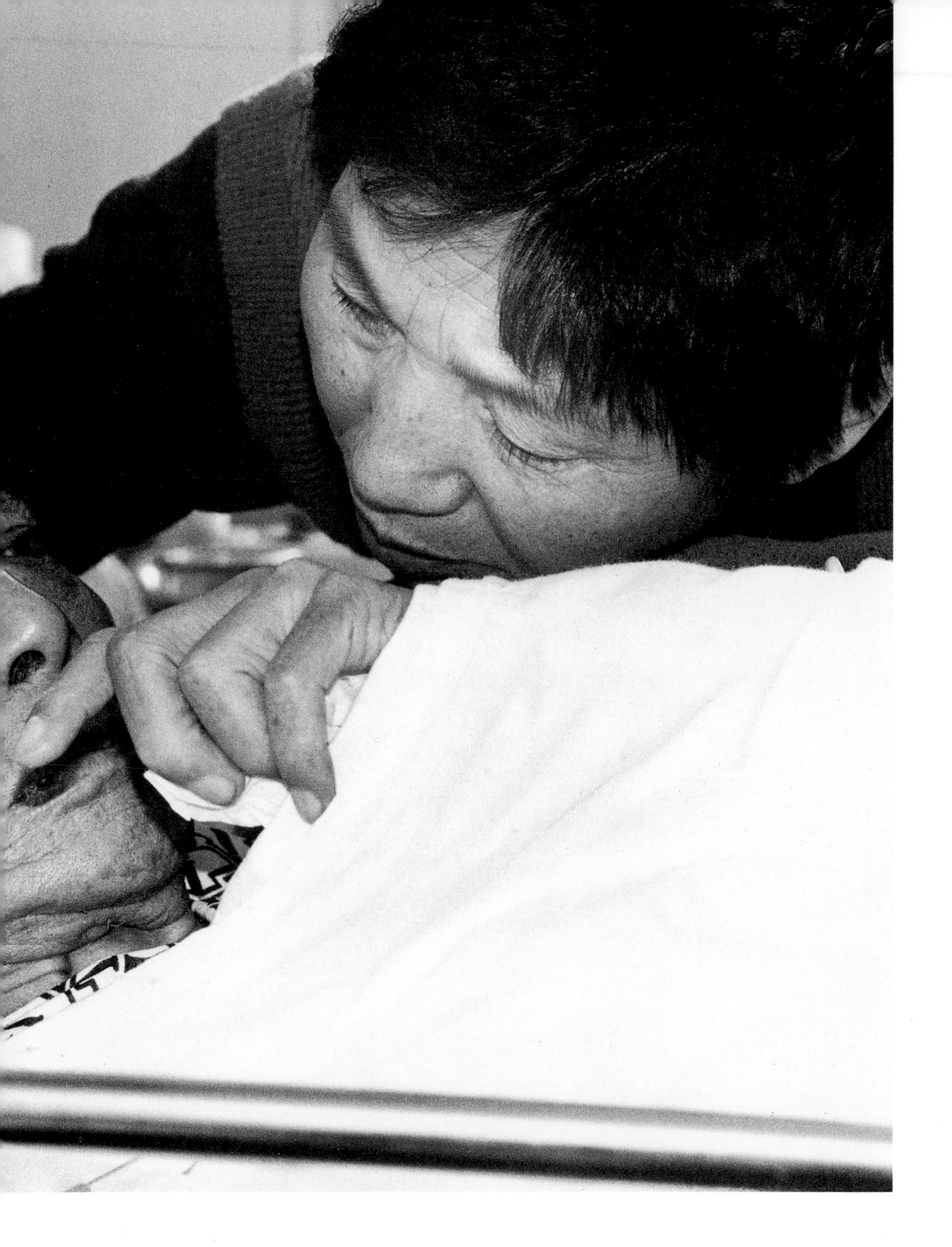

Tears come into his eyes and those of his wife. He had hoped to defeat the bomb in his lifetime, but now Nature threatens to silence his voice before his mission is accomplished.

Hiromu Morishita has been trying to prove that the brush can be mightier than the sword as he teaches his calligraphy students the grace of writing poetry on anti-war themes.

At first glance, you want to turn away from him. You feel embarrassed, even guilty. The bomb branded one side of his head and melted his left ear "like a candle" when he was a student in the demolition squad in the center of the city.

But then you are attracted by the inner beauty of this man who is both poet and calligrapher, as he tells you that his only salvation has been to work for peace in a personal way. He and a group of teachers have organized a peace study program, and are charting the children's changing attitudes to nuclear issues like a moral fever chart.

"I shall keep working as long as nations are threatened by war," he says. "The hope of the world lies with the young. They must realize the danger before it is too late."

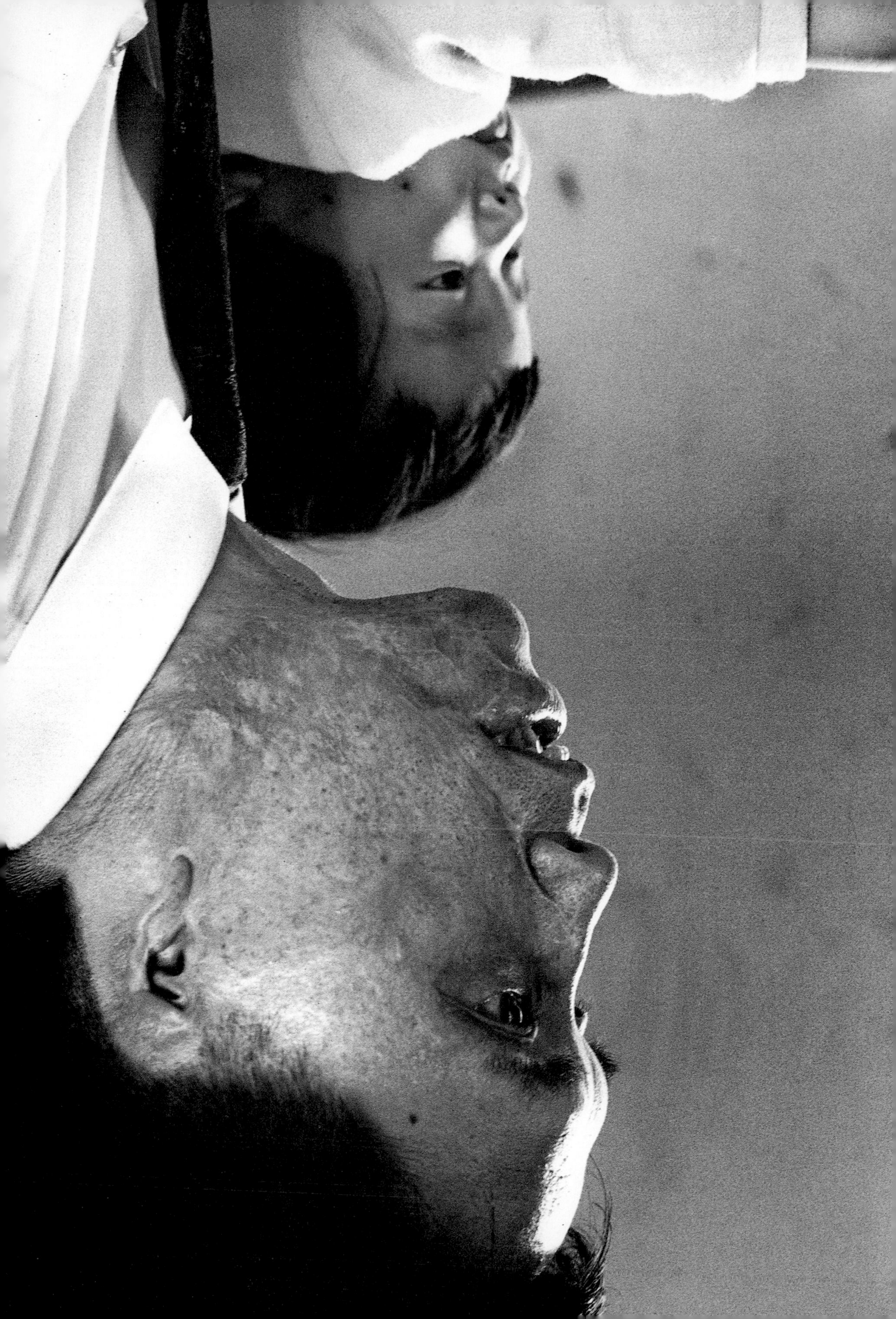

Michiko Yamaoka was known as a "Hiroshima Maiden" when she and twenty-five other badly disfigured young women were flown to New York to be operated on in the mid-fifties. The surgeons could not completely restore what the bomb had destroyed, but they could hope to rebuild inner confidence while working on what had once been eyelids, noses, mouths, and chins.

At fourteen Michiko was half a mile from the hypocenter when she was pinned under the debris of a stone wall. Rescued by her badly injured mother who spotted her feet, she began a nightmarish existence of hospitalizations alternating with reclusive periods in the house her mother assembled piecemeal over the years. She dreaded the taunts of the neighborhood children who shouted "Goblin! Ogre!" when they spotted her macabre form: her head bent, as if melted into her shoulder, her features running into each other with little demarkation, her fingers distorted into claws.

After Michiko's return from America where she had learned to apply makeup to ambiguous areas of her face, as well as professional dressmaking, Michiko struggled to keep her spirits up while nursing her mother who became increasingly debilitated with kidney, liver, and heart problems. Her mother insisted she would not die until Michiko married, for she didn't want her to be alone.

But Michiko, unlike some of the Hiroshima Maidens, did not marry. She felt suicidal when her mother died, spending long periods alone in their tiny house which is now dwarfed by tall modern buildings that block out the sunlight. When people would remind her that she was lucky to have been operated on in America, she would remind them that she would have been even luckier if she were not a victim of the bomb. This past year she has undergone surgery for breast cancer, another reminder of the legacy of radiation.

However, recently, with the help of a dedicated social worker at the A-Bomb Hospital who has been working with *hibakusha*, Michiko has rallied her inner strength, and forced herself to begin speaking to groups of children on school excursions. Although each public appearance is torture to her, she has come to realize that only by speaking out about her experience to the young, can she hope to prevent others from sharing her fate.

4-28

He is known as the "Human Reactor."

Whenever there is a bomb test anywhere in the world, you will find Ichiro Moritake sitting in front of the Cenotaph with a group of students, housewives, workers, Buddhists, and anyone who wants to join their one hour protest.

Moritake, a retired professor of philosophy at Hiroshima University, began the movement by sitting alone. He likes to tell of the little girl who stared at him for a long time, and asked: "Can you stop it by sitting?"

"A chain reaction of spiritual atoms must defeat a chain reaction of material atoms," he responded then, and although many countries are still testing, he would still give the same reply.

Moritake was badly injured and lost his right eye in his own encounter with what he refers to as "the little bomb" that destroyed his city. Since then he has been actively working for increased health benefits for survivors, and national compensation for families of the dead.

He uses his right eye to illustrate his case.

"I never received anything from the government for the loss of my right eye, not even an apology. But when my left eye has problems, I get free medical care. My right eye, then, represents the victims of the bomb—those who were killed and maimed and lost their loved ones. The problem of my right eye can only be solved by national compensation."

核実験反対

"When will your group sit again?" you ask.

"It is not I who determines that," he tells you, "but the governments who test. As long as they continue, we will sit here bearing on our shoulders the burden of all A-Bomb victims—those who died on August 6, those who died later from radiation effects, those who are dying now, those who committed suicide, those who lost loved ones, and those who will suffer genetic effects in the future."